I, TUT

I, TUT

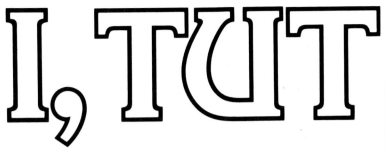

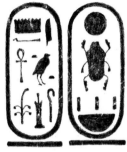

The Boy Who Became Pharaoh

by MIRIAM SCHLEIN

illustrations by
ERIK HILGERDT

Four Winds Press   New York

I would like to express my thanks to Dr. Robert S. Bianchi, Associate
Curator, Department of Egyptian and Classical Art, The Brooklyn Museum,
for reading the manuscript and making helpful suggestions.

Readers may be interested to know that the drawings
on pages 3, 5, and 32 are cartouches which show Tutankhamun's
personal and throne names. His personal name includes the hieroglyph
of a bird, while his throne name includes the hieroglyph of
a scarab. A cartouche of his throne name is shown on the jacket.

Library of Congress Cataloging in Publication Data
Schlein, Miriam.
I, Tut.
Bibliography: p.
1. Tutankhamen, King of Egypt—Juvenile literature.
2. Pharaohs—Biography—Juvenile literature.
I. Hilgerdt, Erik. II. Title.
DT87.5.S3   932'.01'0924   [B]   78-15603
ISBN 0-590-07571-3

Book design by Kathleen Westray

Published by Four Winds Press
A division of Scholastic Magazines, Inc., New York, N.Y.
Text copyright © 1979 by Miriam Schlein
Illustrations copyright © 1979 by Erik Hilgerdt
All rights reserved
Printed in the United States of America
Library of Congress Catalog Card Number: 78-15603

1 2 3 4 5 83 82 81 80 79

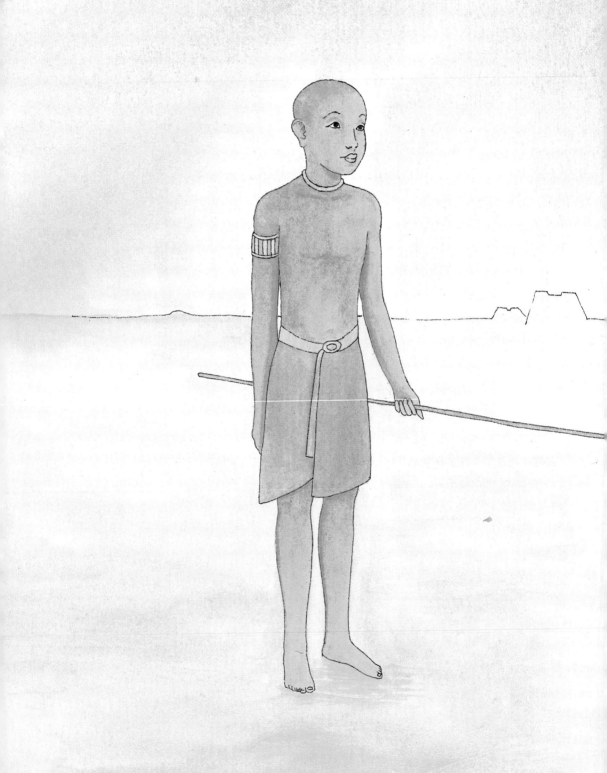

≡ Am I a lucky boy?

I do not know.

My mother tells me I am.

My name is Tutankhaton. It is easier if you just call me Tut.

My father is pharaoh, king of Egypt. His name is Amenhotep III. People call him Amenhotep the Magnificent.

My brother is also pharaoh. My father is getting old, and my brother helps him to rule.

My brother is also called Amenhotep. He is Amenhotep IV.

All this means I am a prince.

Does that make me lucky?

I do not know.

My mother tells me I must grow up to be brave and smart.

≣ A few days ago, it was my birthday. I am six now. On that day, there was a celebration for me in the palace. I did not have to go to school. But every other day, I go to school. The school is right here at the palace.

I have been going since I was four. I am learning to write. And to add up numbers. I am already expected to know many of the hieroglyphs that stand for real and living things. It is hard to remember everything.

Many days, I would rather sit out under the sycamore tree in the garden, with my three spotted dogs — Neb, Abu, and Ken. But every single morning there is school.

I wonder why my mother says I am a lucky boy. (My mother's name is Tiya. She is the queen.)

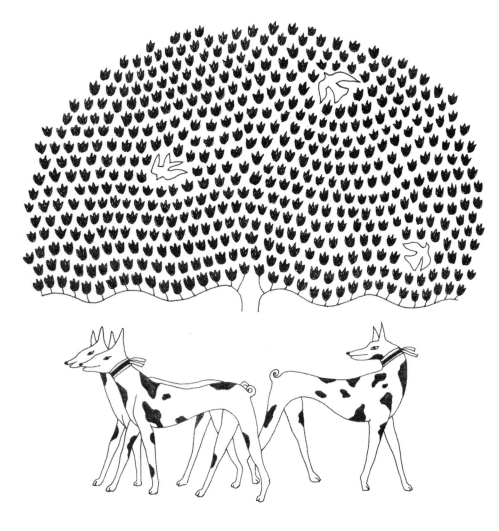

≣ There are some other princes at the palace, here in Thebes. We all do our lessons together. My favorite friend is Hekenefer. He is a prince, too. He is from Nubia, a land far up the Nile, beyond the great cataracts. They have wonderful animals there — giraffes, elephants. He tells me about them. Some day I would like to go and see them myself....

(My mother Tiya is from Nubia. But she does not remember much about it. She came here to the north when she was a little girl.)

▤ There are five of us here at school. We sit on the floor, our legs crossed, our palettes on our laps. We sit straight and steady, just like scribes. We dip our small reed pens in the ink, and write. Today we are copying the story of the shipwrecked sailor and the serpent. I work carefully. I like to copy stories.

The teacher comes and leans over us. "Yes, yes, very good," he says. Then he says, "No." In red ink, he goes over my hieroglyph of the serpent.

Now I must correct it. I take my sandstone eraser from its little leather sack. I rub gently, then smooth the papyrus so I can write on that spot again.

"Remember, boys," says the teacher, "what you gain in one day at school is for eternity. The work done here is as lasting as mountains."

How many times have we heard him say this? Three hundred. At least!

I peek up at Hekenefer. Hekenefer peeks up at me. We just barely keep ourselves from laughing.

There is one good thing about hearing our teacher say this: Generally, it means that our morning's work is just about over.

≣ In the afternoon, there is no school. We can do things we like to do. We have wrestling contests in the courtyard, or we swim in the pool.

Some days I just like to have a quiet game of senet with a friend under the sycamore tree in the garden.

Other times, the master-at-arms takes me out to hunt in the desert. We set out in a chariot, with bows and arrows.

These are the creatures I have shot, so far:

A gazelle.

An ostrich. (Its feathers were used as plumes for my fan.)

Some little rabbits. They did not know which way to run. So they stood still. I killed them.

Is this what my mother means by being brave? They say my father, when he was young and strong, was a great hunter. My brother Amenhotep IV is not.

I have another brother, too. His name is Smenkhkare. He is older than I am. But, Amenhotep IV — my brother who is pharaoh — is older than both of us.

He thinks about animals, and he writes about them and he puts them in his hymn to the sun-god Aton; but he does not enjoy the hunt. He wrote this:

> *All cattle rest upon their pasturage,*
> *The trees and plants flourish,*
> *The birds flutter in their marshes,*
> *Their wings uplifted in adoration to thee.*
> *All the sheep dance upon their feet,*
> *All winged things fly.*
> *They live when thou [the sun] hast shone*
> *   upon them.*

I like that, about how the sheep dance upon their feet.

I wonder: If a man does not like to hunt, does that mean he is not brave?

≡ I do not see my pharaoh-brother very much. He lives in a different city, far to the north. It is a new city; my brother had it built for himself, in the sand where there once was nothing.

It is a beautiful city. He lives there with his queen Nefertiti, and their daughters. He calls his city Akhetaton. It is named for Aton, the god of the sun. It means "Horizon of Aton." Sometimes it is called the City of the Disc (the round disc being the sun).

I went to visit there once, when I was three. We went in the royal barge. It was several days' travel, down the Nile. We all went: my father Amenhotep, my mother Tiya, my sister Bake-taten, Smenkhkare — and me.

In the streets of Akhetaton there was a parade. I rode in it, in a gold chariot, with the princess Ankhesenpaaten.

The vizier was running beside us. He was puffing to keep up. He had such a big belly.

I remember it all — though I was only three.

And I remember we went to pray to the sun-god Aton, in a beautiful temple, open to the rays of the sun.

≡ In Egypt, we have many gods.

There is Osiris, the god of the underworld, the Land of the Dead, where all people go when they die.

There is the moon-god, Thoth, the god of learning, the god of the scribes.

There is Bes. He is the god of childbirth. He keeps sickness away.

There is Anubis, the jackal. He is the god of mummification. (That is the way the body of a dead person is preserved and made into a mummy.)

Another is the goddess Isis, the wife of Osiris, and mother of the universe.

In Thebes, where I live, the most important god is Amun, the god of the wind, of the atmosphere around us. Amun is the official state god of Egypt.

We have sacred animals, too, which represent the gods — the ram, the crocodile, the baboon, the cat, and others.

People pray to all these gods. And we have many statues of them.

≡ Time has gone by. My father Amenhotep the Magnificent is dead. He was buried in a great burial chamber in the side of the mountain, in the Valley of the Kings. He has gone to Osiris in the Land of the Dead, where he will no longer be old and sick. In the Land of the Dead, he will be young again; he will be young forever.

≡ Strange things are happening here in Thebes. Soldiers are breaking up the statues of the gods. The temple of Amun has been closed. Even statues of our father Amenhotep have been broken with hammers and chisels, so that the name of the god Amun is wiped out of sight everywhere.

They say these things are done under the orders of my brother, the pharaoh.

My brother says all life comes from the sun-god, Aton. And he will not allow anybody to worship Amun or any of the other gods anymore.

My brother has even changed his own name. He is no longer called Amenhotep, like our father. (For that name honors Amun. It means "Amun is content." And my brother does not wish to honor Amun.)

The new name he has given himself is Akhenaton. It means "he who is agreeable to Aton."

The people are not happy about this. The priests are very bitter, and hate my brother.

All day I hear shouting from the streets of the city. But now, at a quiet moment, I hear the roar of a lion in the desert.

Many things in Egypt are changing.

≡ Thousands of people used to work for the priesthood of Amun. They worked in fields, and they worked in shops. They grew things, and they made things. Some sailed on ships and traded with foreign lands. All of this was managed by the priesthood.

Now my brother has taken the priests' power away. Everything is in confusion.

It is said that people are praying to the old gods in secret. It is said, too, that the priests are just waiting for the time when they can become powerful once again.

≡ My friend Hekenefer has heard that enemies of Egypt are sweeping into our lands at the border. But my pharaoh-brother does nothing. Does he not know any of these things? Does he not care?

He just stays up there, in his new City of the Disc. He swears he will never leave it.

People are saying he is crazy.

≡ I guess he knows he needs help. Akhenaton has made our brother Smenkhkare co-regent, to help him rule. My two brothers are now pharaohs!

Akhenaton still stays in the City of the Disc. Smenkhkare is going to rule from Thebes, where most of the trouble is.

Nefertiti is no longer Akhenaton's queen. He has sent her away from his palace. She now lives with some of her daughters in another palace in the northern part of the City of the Disc. I spend a good deal of time there.

≡ It has been decided that I, Tut, am to marry Ankhesenpaaten.

She is the third daughter of Akhenaton and Nefertiti. I have known her my whole life. Relatives in the royal family often marry each other.

I am eight years old. She is eleven.

▤ We have been married one year now. We live in the north palace with Nefertiti. It is quiet here.

But the quiet days were soon over. I remember the day well when my life changed. We were in the garden — Ankhesenpaaten and I. She had picked two little bouquets for me, of lotuses and poppies. She was just handing them to me when we heard people running about in the palace. We went in to see what was happening. Then we found out the news.

Akhenaton and Smenkhkare were both dead. Both my brothers. What had happened to them? It was hard to find out. No one seemed to know. At least, no one seemed to want to tell me.

Who will be pharaoh now?

≡ I have not had much time to write, these days. I had to get ready for yesterday. There were suddenly many new things I had to learn and remember.

Yesterday was the coronation.

The new pharaoh of Egypt was crowned.

I, Tut, am the new pharaoh.

Perhaps now I should use my whole name.

I, Tutankhaton, am the pharaoh.

I am nine years old.

I was made pharaoh because I am the son of a pharaoh, and my wife is daughter of a pharaoh. There are no other men left in the royal family but me.

There is so much for me to learn. Ay, the vizier, and the general Horemheb are helping me.

The coronation was at the temple of Karnak in Thebes. They escorted me there. One on each side of me, we walked to the great pylon, gateway to the temple.

Then they left me. I stood alone, before the temple built by my father not so many years ago.

Priests came, wearing masks of the gods: Horus the falcon, Thoth the ibis, and Seth the dog. They took my hand and led me into the temple.

Inside, I stepped into a shallow pool for purification. Then, from gold pitchers, the priests poured water over me. As Horemheb and Ay had explained to me before, this was to give me divine life; I am now fit to appear before the gods.

A priest dressed as Amun's daughter, the snake goddess, embraced me. Then another priest placed several crowns on my head, one after the other; these gave me the powers and duties of a pharaoh. At that moment, I became pharaoh.

Outside, I rode through the crowds in a gold-and-silver-plated chariot. The people cheered me. "We will have better times now," they cried.

≡ There were important things to be done, even my first day as pharaoh. Horemheb and Ay discussed them with me.

First, amnesty was declared. All prisoners were let out of jail. We would have no more fighting between the followers of Aton and the followers of Amun. We would start anew.

≡ Before I left Thebes, I was asked to inspect a statue of me, with Amun, that the artists have already begun to carve.

Then Ankhesenpaaten and I left Thebes to go home.

The old man Ay is called the "Divine Father." For many years he has been adviser to pharaohs — first to my father, then to my brother. I am lucky to have him to advise me. He is to be my vizier. He accompanied us back to the City of the Disc.

≡ I have been pharaoh for more than a year now.

When I first became pharaoh, the land was topsy-turvy. The temples of the gods were broken ruins. Weeds were growing inside them. People took shortcuts through these once-sacred places. Dogs ran and played in the rubble.

Because of this, the gods turned their backs on our land. There was hunger and hate and confusion. Our great land of Egypt was not great anymore.

Things are different, since I am on the throne.

I have reopened trade with Byblos. Great cedar trees are again being shipped to us by river. They are used to make new barges for the gods. The barges are painted gold so they may once again light up the Nile with their glow.

I have not just stayed here at the palace. I have traveled up and down our land, from the Elephantine to the Delta. I have visited the rebuilt temples.

I have had jeweled statues of the ancient gods set up.

No other pharaoh as young as I has caused so much to be built in so short a time.

People are now allowed to pray again to Amun and the rest of the gods. At home, I myself pray to Isis, and leave flowers for Amun. Yet, I have not turned my back on Aton, my pharaoh-brother's one god, the sun-god.

I grew up a believer in Aton. His name is even in my name — Tutankh*aton*. And so, on one side of my throne is carved AMUN. Yet on the other side is carved ATON.

My royal scepter also has ATON carved upon it.

I think there is room in Egypt for many gods.

I am proud of all I have done in just one year.

≣ It is funny. Even though I am pharaoh of Egypt, I still must go to school. It is not the way it used to be. I am not in a class now. I study alone, with a tutor.

Thinking of those days makes me think of Hekenefer. I have not seen my friend since he returned to Nubia, several years ago.

The things I learn now are more complicated. Here are some of the questions I must answer:

How many men are needed to transport an obelisk 60 cubits* long? How large a ramp is needed to raise it?

I am taught how to plan a military expedition. And I have to study the geography of foreign lands. I can add and subtract fractions. I can calculate the area of a triangle.

My tutor says I am doing well. I will soon be finishing my second cycle of studies. When I do, I will be known as "a scribe who has received the writing case."

I remember my mother saying I must grow up to be strong and smart. Was this what she was thinking — that one day I might become pharaoh?

*A cubit was a unit of measurement—the distance from a man's elbow to his middle finger. It was about 20 inches.

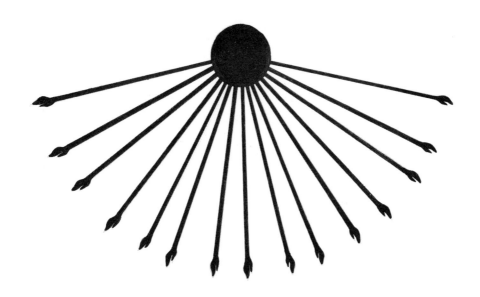

☰ We are moving.

I am now in the fourth year of my reign. We have lived these four years in the north palace in Akhetaton. But Horemheb and Ay both feel it would be better if I ruled from Thebes. Thebes is the largest city, and the richest. It is known as a great city not only in Egypt, but all over the world. The powerful priesthood of Amun is in Thebes. It is where the important things happen.

And so, we are moving to Thebes.

Men are moving our furniture onto barges. They will be taken up the Nile to Thebes.

I am going to look around here once more. I wonder: Will I ever see the City of the Disc again?*

*It is believed that Tut never did return to Akhetaton (the City of the Disc).

▤ What is my name?

Who am I?

When I was born, I was given the name Tut-ankhaton. It is a name that honors Aton. It means "perfect is the life of Aton."

My wife was given the name Ankhesenpaaten. That means "her life is Aton's."

Horemheb wants us to change our names. He says times have changed.

Aton is no longer the only god. The priest-hood of the god Amun is again very strong and rich. When my brother was pharaoh, he tried to destroy them, in the name of Aton. Now the name of Aton offends them.

It would be better, Horemheb says, if our names were to honor Amun, instead of Aton.

From now on, in this fourth year of my reign, I am to be known as Tutankhamun, "perfect is the life of Amun." My queen-wife is now called Ankhesenamun, "may she live for Amun."

≡ In Thebes, there was a great festival to honor Amun, called the Feast of Opet. I took part in it. First, the priests, all in white, carried high from the temple little barges and shrines for the gods. I followed them. Music played as we came forth.

They placed the shrines on a sacred barge bright with gold and jewels. Then I picked up an oar. I really did not have to row; this was just the signal to begin. People on the riverbank sang, danced, and carried pennants high, as men towed the barges upriver to Luxor. There it was like a big party. People from all over Egypt had come to celebrate. Peasants, soldiers, workmen, men, women, children, old and young, people of every rank, high and low, were here.

To the sound of drums and trumpets, Nubian tribesmen danced naked with their spears. There were jugglers and acrobats doing tricks to the rhythm of castanets. There was food, and drink, and tables were piled high with offerings to all the gods — geese, honey cake, fruit, wine, incense, and flowers.

Every day the crowds of people ate up 11,341 loaves of bread, and drank 385 jugs of beer.

Eleven days the celebration went on. On the last day, great fat oxen with gilded horns were sacrificed to the gods, so that the sacred barge might make a safe trip back down to the temple of Karnak.

People enjoy such festivals. They did not have them when my brother was pharaoh.

It is over now. From the palace roof, I can see Sothis, the dog-star, up in the sky. I can see in the distance the fields flooded over by the Nile. The moon shines on the water. When flood-time is over, farmers will plant on their rich fields. Oxen will pull the plows.

The gods are good to Egypt.

The feast is over.

Everyone is tired.

≡ I have been told that grave robbers have broken into the tombs of my ancestors. They took gold statues and jewelry which had been placed in the tomb for my ancestors to use in the Land of the Dead. I myself went to the Valley of the Kings to see the damage. I have ordered repairs to be made, and for the tombs to be guarded more closely.

≡ I have been pharaoh for eight years now. I have learned how to rule from Ay and from the general Horemheb.

Horemheb deals with business and military matters. He sees that taxes are collected from Palestine and Lebanon. His troops protected the people of Palestine when enemies swept into their land.

I myself write to and meet with foreign princes and kings. I know it is important not to let our enemies join together and become too strong.

I have not seen it, but I have been told that Horemheb has had an inscription placed on a wall. It says that he, Horemheb, is "the greatest of the great, the most powerful of the powerful, high lord of the people...."

He must remember that it is *I* who am pharaoh. He is only my general.

I am closer to Ay, my vizier, who stays at the palace.

 Today was a happy day. I had been looking forward to it. Many princes have come from the south, to pay tribute to Egypt. They came in many barges and boats. How busy the waterfront must have been when they arrived.

I, Tut, sat under a canopy to receive their gifts. Beautiful things piled up before me — gold rings, bags of gold dust, elephant tusks, throw sticks made of ebony, shields covered in animal skin. How I longed to get down to touch and examine these beautiful things. But Ay told me beforehand I must keep a dignified manner. So I did not move.

Three princes of Wawat were led up to me. On their heads they wore ostrich plumes, set in headbands. They bowed low. When they arose, I saw that one of the princes was Hekenefer.

How difficult it was for me to keep a dignified manner. How I longed to jump down and embrace my old friend. How fine he looked. Tall and strong.

As he looked at me, he blinked his eyes fast, a funny thing he used to do. I nearly laughed. But I did not. I must be more dignified now.

Now I was eager for the ceremony to be finished, so that I could talk to Hekenefer, and clasp his hand.

More gifts were placed before me. Beautiful carved furniture of wood with fur cushions. Great bows and arrows. And a gold-plated chariot.

The most marvelous gift came last, from the land of Kush. It would not enrich our treasury, or provide gold to make great statues of Amun. But it was my favorite. It was a giraffe. What a beautiful animal it is. She came toward me, with a most stately walk. Then she was led away.

Later on I spent much time with Hekenefer. It was not like the old days, when we wrestled and joked and ran with my dogs, and played senet under the sycamore tree in the garden.

Still—this has been one of the nicest days of my life.

■ My name is Hekenefer. I shall have to tell the end of this story. My good friend Tut is no longer here to do so.

He was eighteen years old when he died. He had been pharaoh for half his life. He was gentle, and bright. The people of Egypt went on their knees and wept when he died.

It is not known how he died. But it was sudden. Was he struck down by an enemy — a traitor — someone in the court whom he trusted, but who was really an enemy? Or did he get a sudden illness? Not even I, an old friend, can find out.

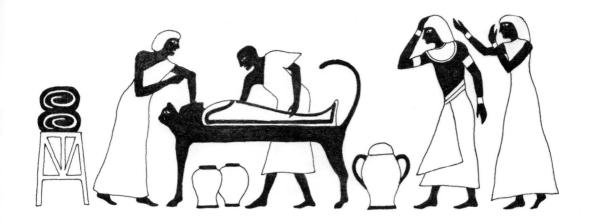

≡ It took seventy days to prepare his body as a mummy, so that he may live forever in the Land of the Dead. They withdrew his brains through his nose. They cut his body, and removed his intestines.

He was wrapped in linen. Jewels and flowers were thrown over him. Then his body was laid on a sledge. Red oxen pulled it to the temple.

In his gold coffin, he was laid to rest in the Valley of the Kings, near his father. The doors were sealed, and the tomb walled in.

At nightfall, torches were lit, and a tent erected. We had a funeral banquet outside as Tut, alone in his tomb, found his way to eternal life, in the Land of the Dead.

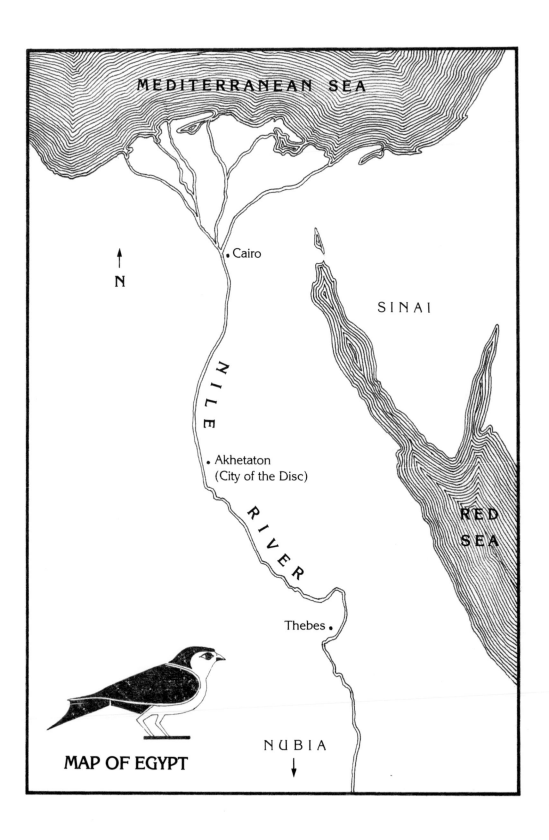

MEDITERRANEAN SEA

N

Cairo

SINAI

NILE

Akhetaton
(City of the Disc)

RIVER

RED
SEA

Thebes

MAP OF EGYPT

NUBIA

≡ AUTHOR'S NOTES ≡

The people in this book were all real people who lived in ancient Egypt about 3,300 years ago. Although we know a lot about Tut's time — from archaeological findings, from documents and stories and letters written in hieroglyphics which we have been able to decipher — it is still one of the puzzles of history that we do not know exactly who Tut was. That is, who his mother and father were.

Many experts who have studied this period hold the view that Tut was the son of Amenhotep III and the queen Tiya, and that Akhenaton and Smenkhkare were Tut's older brothers. (This is the relationship we have accepted for this book.)

As a basis for this belief, Egyptologists point to some pieces of evidence found in Tut's tomb — a small gold statue of Amenhotep III, and a lock of Tiya's hair. In addition, an inscription on a monument has been found in which Tut calls Amenhotep III his father. They also point out that Tut resembled Tiya very closely.

Other Egyptologists say that these items in Tut's tomb don't prove anything at all, and that in the inscription in which Tut calls Amenhotep III his "father," they feel he is using the word in a very general sense, simply meaning his ancestor.

Still others believe that Tut's father was Amenhotep III, but that his mother was not Tiya, but a secondary wife. (It was customary for pharaohs to have numerous additional wives.) Others think that Tiya was Tut's mother, but that Amenhotep III was not his father.

There was a big age difference between Tut and Akhenaton, and some Egyptologists think that Akhenaton was Tut's father, not his brother.

There is even one theory that when Akhenaton made Smenkhkare co-regent to help him rule, it was not Smenkhkare who went to Thebes, but Queen Nefertiti in disguise.

Some day, if more discoveries are made, we may have better answers to these questions.

In some places you may see these names spelled in different ways. Tutankhamun is sometimes spelled Tutankhamon, or Tutankhamen.

Amenhotep III (Tut's father) is sometimes called Amenhotpe III or Amenophis III.

Akhenaton (Tut's brother) is sometimes spelled Akhenaten or Ikhanaton.

The new city he built — Akhetaton, or the City of the Disc — is often called Amarna.

Nefertiti is sometimes Nafertiti.

Tiya is sometimes Tiye or Teye.

Hekenefer is sometimes spelled Hiknefer.

Amun is sometimes written Amon; Aton sometimes Aten.

The names may also be translated in somewhat different ways. Some scholars say Tutankhaton means "perfect is the life of Aton." Others feel it is closer in meaning to "the living image of Aton."

Some scholars translate Akhenaton to mean "Aton is satisfied," or "he in whom Aton is satisfied." Other translations sometimes given are "the incarnation of Aton," or "it goes well with the Aton," or "he who is agreeable to the Aton."

We do not know the exact dates of Tut's rule. They are given variously as:

1334 B.C. to 1325 B.C.

1369 B.C. to 1360 B.C.

1352 B.C. to 1344 B.C.

1357 B.C. to 1350 B.C.

It is generally agreed that Tut was on the throne seven or eight or nine years. When he died, he was still in his teens.

▤ HOW TO PRONOUNCE THE NAMES ▤

Stress the part of the name that is underlined.

Akhenaton — Ah-ken-ah-ton

Akhetaton — Ah-ket-ah-ton

Amenhotep — Ah-men-ho-tep

Amun — Ah-mun

Ankhesenamun — Onk-es-en-ah-mun

Ankhesenpaaten — Onk-es-en-pa-ah-ten

Anubis — A-new-bis

Aton — Ah-ton

Baketaten — Bak-et-ah-ten

Hekenefer — Heck-en-efer

Horemheb — Ho-rem-heb

Nefertiti — Ne-fer-tee-tee

Nubia — New-bia

Osiris — O-sigh-rus

Pharaoh — Fay-row

Smenkhkare — Smenk-car-ay

Tiya — Tee-uh

Tutankhamun — Tut-onk-ah-mun

Tutankhaton — Tut-onk-ah-ton

≡ BIBLIOGRAPHY ≡

Aldred, Cyril. *Akhenaten, Pharaoh of Egypt —A New Study.* New York: McGraw-Hill Book Company, 1968.

Cottrel, Leonard. *The Lost Pharaohs.* New York: Holt, Rinehart and Winston, Inc., 1961.

Harris, J.R., ed. *The Legacy of Egypt.* London: Oxford University Press, 1971.

Hawkes, Jacquetta. *Pharaohs of Egypt.* New York: American Heritage Publishing Company, 1965.

Metropolitan Museum of Art. *Treasures of Tutankhamun.* New York, 1976.

Montet, Pierre. *Lives of the Pharaohs.* Cleveland: The World Publishing Company, 1968.

Noblecourt, Christiane Desroches-. *Tutankhamen.* London: George Rainbird Ltd., 1963.

Riefstahl, Elizabeth. *Thebes in the Time of Amunhotep III.* Norman, Oklahoma: University of Oklahoma Press, 1964.

Wiley-el-dine Sameh. *Daily Life in Ancient Egypt.* Translated by Michael Bullock. New York: McGraw-Hill Book Company, 1964.

Wilson, John A. *The Burden of Egypt.* Chicago: University of Chicago Press, 1951.